JARROLD SHORT WALKS

Compiled by
David Foster

JARROLD
publishing

Mapping
sourced from
Ordnance
Survey

Acknowledgements

Among the people who helped me research this book, I must mention Lee Skinner, of Isle of Wight Council's Rights of Way Department, and Tom Ransom, of Forest Enterprise. Robin Lang and Ian Ridett, of the National Trust, guided me through the difficult terrain at St Catherine's, and Colonel Aylmer kindly allowed me to photograph his home at Nunwell House. On a domestic note, Olive Glass, of Red Funnel, and Susan Hemmings, of WightLink, made sure that my travel arrangements ran without a hitch. And, by no means least, I have fond memories of warm hospitality from Alisson and Jim Smith at Field House, Freshwater, and Peter and Jackie at the Shangri-La Hotel, Sandown.

Text: David Foster
Photography: David Foster
Editor: Crawford Gillan
Designer: Sarah Crouch

© Jarrold Publishing 2004

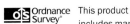 This product includes mapping data licensed from Ordnance Survey® with the permission of the Controller of Her Majesty's Stationery Office. © Crown Copyright 2003. All rights reserved. Licence number 100017593. Ordnance Survey, the OS symbol and Pathfinder are registered trademarks and Explorer, Landranger and Outdoor Leisure are trademarks of the Ordnance Survey, the national mapping agency of Great Britain.

Jarrold Publishing ISBN 0-7117-3007-5

First published 2004
by Jarrold Publishing

Printed in Belgium
by Proost NV, Turnhout. 1/04

Jarrold Publishing
Pathfinder Guides, Whitefriars, Norwich NR3 1JR
E-mail: info@totalwalking.co.uk
www.totalwalking.co.uk

Front cover: Newtown High Street
Previous page: Alum Bay

Contents

Keymap

SCALE 1:384 615 or 1 INCH to about 6 MILES *1CM to 3.8KM*

0   2   4   6   8   10 KILOMETRES   15

0   2   4   6   MILES 8   10

KEYMAP HEIGHTS SHOWN IN FEET

Introduction

Beyond Freshwater, the great white cliffs rise sheer from the English Channel. Here, the island narrows to a frail peninsula as the chalk ridge that stretches almost unbroken from its eastern extremity at Culver Cliff romps westwards over Tennyson Down to the Needles.

From his home at nearby Farringford, the Victorian poet laureate Alfred, Lord Tennyson, declared that the downland air was worth sixpence a pint. In today's money the price would be rather higher, for this is magical stuff. To be truthful, stepping out onto the coastal path in the golden light of a summer's evening is something like flying; your feet move easily over the close-cropped turf and, as you soar skywards on the westerly breeze, you can see almost 40 miles (64km) from Swanage to St Catherine's Point.

Inspiring landscapes

With its dramatic cliffs, wide-open river estuaries and rolling chalk downland, the Isle of Wight offers some of Britain's most diverse countryside. Ringed by nearly 30 miles (48km) of 'Heritage coasts', more than half the island is officially designated as being of outstanding natural beauty. Away from the bustling seaside resorts, you'll find pretty lanes and thatched villages just waiting to welcome you – and, it's said, there's a pub for almost every square mile on the island.

More than 500 miles (805km) of carefully maintained footpaths make this the perfect destination for walkers. Here, walking is part of the culture. Eight waymarked leisure trails link the interior to the island's 67-mile (108km) coast path, and the Isle of Wight Council was the first authority in England to

Crossing Niton Down

St Agnes' Church, Freshwater Bay

meet the Government's national rights-of-way target. No wonder some 25,000 people descend on the island each May for the UK's biggest walking festival, sponsored by Red Funnel ferries.

Turbulent times

Long before these modern invasions, the island was captured by Vespasian and absorbed into the Roman Empire in the middle of the first century. The Romans built villas like the ones at Brading and Newport. They called their new territory Vectis – a name that you'll see every day on the side of Southern Vectis buses.

After the Romans left Britain some 400 years later, their place was taken by the West Saxons. The islanders endured foreign raids throughout this turbulent period until, in 1066, the Norman Conquest heralded an era of political stability. King William's military commander founded the castle at Carisbrooke, as well as a number of island churches including the distinctive All Saints at Newchurch.

Years later, in 1256, the church itself took a hand in the island's development when the Bishop of Winchester established the port of Newtown. The town quickly grew prosperous and, for a time, it was the busiest port on the island; later, it fell victim to the old problem of foreign raids when the French destroyed it in 1377.

Further French incursions in the 16th century prompted Henry VIII to defend the island with a chain of forts such as the one at Yarmouth. History repeated itself in the Victorian era, and the government embarked on an extensive network of fortifications to protect Portsmouth's naval base from the old enemy. Island defences like the patriotically named Fort Victoria and Fort Albert were built to support a string of forts on the mainland and at Spithead.

A wildlife stronghold

If the Isle of Wight has borne its share of foreign invasions, it has so far remained secure against a more insidious assault. The American grey squirrel was introduced to Britain in the 1870s and, by the mid-20th century, it had driven native red squirrels from most parts of the mainland. Today, the Isle of Wight is one of the few places in southern England where you can see this engaging creature in its natural habitat.

The island is also the last British stronghold of the attractive Glanville fritillary butterfly, and a small colony of reddish-buff moths near Newtown Harbour is the only native population of its kind anywhere in Britain. Low-lying estuaries and mudflats at Newtown, Yarmouth and along the Medina are great places for wildlife, and birdwatchers may see waterfowl such as little egret, curlew, redshank or black-tailed godwit.

In fact, the island is something of a naturalist's paradise. The southern coastline contains more than 20 miles (32km) of naturally developing soft cliffs, an internationally rare habitat protected by European legislation. Often called the Dinosaur Coast, this crumbling coastline is rich in fossils, as well as rare insects and colourful plants like field cow-wheat, hoary stock and ivy broomrape.

Winners and losers

You'll witness the dramatic effects of this natural erosion on several of the walks, and it's not surprising that coastal protection is a thorny issue on an island that has been changing its shape since prehistoric times. Realigning the coastal path may be relatively straightforward, but regular landslips also threaten sections of the Military Road between Niton and Freshwater.

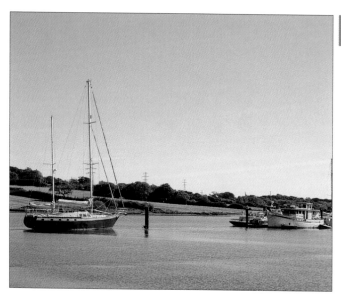

Moorings on the River Medina

Attractions like Isle of Wight Pearl stand close to the retreating cliffs and the gardens at Blackgang Chine are now much smaller than when they were first laid out in the 1840s. In contrast, the inland walks will bring you to historic buildings like Appuldurcombe House, Bembridge windmill and Newtown town hall that have been saved from collapse through the ravages of time. The Isle of Wight steam railway is another success story, with three times as much track as it had just a few years ago.

With so much to see, you may be wondering where to start. If you're already on the island, you'll probably want to begin with a nearby walk – but don't forget that with up to 350 ferry crossings a day, the Isle of Wight makes a great day out from the mainland. Three of the walks in this book start close to the main ferry terminals, and there are also good public transport links to the rest of the island.

So lace up your boots and dig out the maps – you don't want to miss the boat.

1 To the lighthouse

START Windy Gap car park, Old Blackgang Road

DISTANCE 1¾ miles (2.8km)

TIME 1 hour

PARKING Free at start

ROUTE FEATURES This route may become very muddy and slippery in wet weather, and many paths are not signposted. Camping and fires are prohibited, and visitors should keep dogs on leads

The route begins by dropping down through the contorted National Trust landscape to reach the lighthouse road. There is a pleasant walk through the fields above St Catherine's Point, before joining Castlehaven Lane for the climb to the Buddle Inn. A gentle section along leafy Old Blackgang Road completes the circuit.

Leave the car park by the kissing-gate that was on your left as you drove into the car park, and follow the undulating path for 90 yds (82m). Here, a sea view opens up on your right and there is a shallow valley running away to the left. Turn along the valley, and walk between the rocky outcrops and low trees for 160 yds (146m) until you come to a fork in the path. Keep right here, climbing steeply for a few paces through a gap in the trees, for your first view of the gleaming white lighthouse below. Now bear left and follow the path as it winds along the hillside with good coastal views to your right. Just beyond a small concrete survey pillar the path dives between tall bushes and drops steadily down to a wire fence. Turn right, and continue for the last 60 yds (55m) to a gate and stile leading you out onto the lighthouse road.

Ⓐ Nip over the stile and turn right down the hill, until you reach a large pair of stone gate pillars on the left-hand side. The prominent local Kirkpatrick family built the pillars in the first half of the 19th

PUBLIC TRANSPORT Limited bus service from Ventnor to the Buddle Inn (01983 532373)

REFRESHMENTS The Buddle Inn: real ales, home cooked food, garden

PUBLIC TOILETS None

PICNIC/PLAY AREA None, but opportunities for informal picnics

ORDNANCE SURVEY MAPS Explorer OL29 (Isle of Wight)

century as a grand entrance for a summer residence. However, because of the site's exposed location, the house itself was never built. Instead, the family built Windcliff, farther up the hill, in 1840.

Turn between the pillars and through a kissing-gate onto footpath NT40 towards Castlehaven Lane. Follow the hedge on your left through a second kissing-gate, and continue through a third gate that leads you between hedges for the short remaining distance to Castlehaven Lane. Fork left up the hill, pass the Old Radio Station and Wireless Cottage, and follow the lane as it bears left and climbs to the junction with St Catherine's Road.

> **? Who was the most famous resident of Knowles Farm House?**

Castlehaven is an integral part of the long, unbroken stretch of cliff that runs from Totland to Ventnor, and residents in this area are not immune to the general threat of landslips along the south coast.

Chale Bay and **St Catherine's** was notorious for wrecks, with a record 14 losses on a single night in 1757. Although the 14th-century lighthouse on St Catherine's Hill (see Walk 9) was operational for some 200 years, it was often obscured by fog at the very times when it was most needed. The present lighthouse was built in 1840, following the wreck of the *Clarendon* in 1837. It is open to the public, and guided tours last 20 minutes.

St Catherine's Lighthouse

Several properties have sustained serious damage from subsidence in recent years, and the Military Road recently had to be re-routed around nearby Beauchamp House after it was severed by a major landslip.

Niton Undercliff – the area between the towering inland cliffs and the sea – is one of the most unstable sections of the Island's steadily eroding south-west coastline. Powerful landslips have created the dramatic, contorted scenery, and the constantly disturbed soil is home to many unusual plants and insects. Wild liquorice and tufted centaury both grow on the National Trust's estate, which also supports a colony of the rare Glanville fritillary butterfly.

Work began on a £4.3 million coast protection and drainage scheme in 2003, in an effort to secure the future of homes in Castlehaven. The project includes a 20-acre (8ha) nature reserve to help mitigate the effect on the area's outstanding local wildlife.

B Turn left along St Catherine's Road to the Buddle Inn on your right-hand side. Just here, turn right up the signposted footpath beside the pub garden. Turn left at the top, and follow the road round to its junction with Old Blackgang Road. Turn right, and follow the leafy old road back to the start of your walk.

The old town at Newtown

2

START Old town hall, Newtown

DISTANCE 2 miles (3.2km)

TIME 1 hour

PARKING Free National Trust car park opposite the town hall

ROUTE FEATURES This is easy, level walking, although there are half a dozen stiles. The route may become muddy in wet weather, and the coastal section may flood at the highest tides. *Please keep your dog on a lead throughout the walk*

This varied route weaves its way around the grassy tracks and paths that once formed Newtown's busy thoroughfares. There's a short section on a quiet country road, but for most of the way you'll follow attractive green lanes and waterside paths through the glorious landscape of Newtown Harbour National Nature Reserve.

Turn left out of the car park and, after 80 yds (73m), turn right through the signposted kissing-gate beside the former Francheville Arms. This lovely green lane runs between hedges of dog rose, bramble and willow and was once part of Newtown's High Street. Cross the waymarked stile, then zigzag right and left through a gap in the hedge and continue over a second waymarked stile. Walk through a gap in the hedge straight ahead of you, then simply follow the waymarked route through a small finger of woodland and out over a stile onto a country lane.

Ⓐ Turn left, follow the road around the left-hand bend, and continue for 600 yds (549m) to the next left-hand bend. Jump the stile in front of you here, and continue between the hedges that fringe the former Gold Street, now a pleasant green lane, until you reach the stile at the far end.

PUBLIC TRANSPORT Very limited bus service from Newport and Yarmouth (01983 532373)

REFRESHMENTS None on the route, but the popular New Inn at Shalfleet is just a mile down the road

PUBLIC TOILETS At the start

ORDNANCE SURVEY MAPS Explorer OL29 (Isle of Wight)

What was the rent for a house and garden when Newtown was first established in 1256?

In medieval times, **Newtown** was the Island's principal port. With its prosperous merchants and tradesmen, its salt pans and its oyster fishery, Newtown was assessed at twice the value of Newport. But things changed: the French sacked the town in 1377, the harbour silted up, and the ships came no more. Today, just a handful of houses, a redundant town hall and a network of green lanes are all that are left of Newtown's flourishing past.

B Cross over the stile and, after just a few paces, turn right along the signposted footpath up the gated lane past Marsh Farm House. Continue through a second gate onto a hedged footpath that leads out to the wooden bird hide at the edge of the marsh, where the warden keeps a chalk board list of species seen on the reserve. Take your binoculars, and you may see little egret, pintail and ringed plover – not to mention butterflies like the painted lady and speckled wood.

The old town hall

Newtown quay

Turn left at the hide until, in little more than 100 yds (91m), a small wicket gate brings you to a wooden causeway. Turn left again, go through a kissing-gate, and follow the path up the side of the hay meadows with a hedge on your left-hand side. The path turns left through a second kissing-gate and returns to the road at the Old Coastguard Station, now a private house.

Follow the road around the right-hand bend, briefly retracing your steps at point **B** until the road swings away to the left at the Church of the Holy Spirit. Just here, take the signposted footpath straight ahead, go through a kissing-gate, and bear left across the hay meadows. There's a glorious vista across the Causeway Lake as the path drops down and bears left along the waterfront to a stile. Nip across, and continue for 75 yds (69m) to second stile tucked into the hedge near a bench seat on your left.

C Cross the stile, and turn left up Town Lane to return to the car park opposite the town hall. ●

Newtown's old town hall was an early beneficiary of the mysterious **Ferguson's Gang**. This bizarre band of anonymous National Trust supporters was formed in 1927, and their first project was to raise funds for Shalford Mill in Surrey. The **masked gang members**, who were known by pseudonyms like 'Bill Stickers', 'The Bishop' and 'Red Biddy', bought the town hall for £5 and gave it to the National Trust in 1933. Later, the gang raised £1,000 to restore the building.

3 *Fur and feather at Wroxall*

The walk heads north along the old Ventnor to Shanklin railway line before turning across country through the donkey sanctuary to Freemantle Gate. From here it's easy going to the owl and falcony centre at Appuldurcombe House (see Walk 17), before dropping back down to Wroxall for the short homeward stretch on the old railway.

START St Martins Road, Wroxall

DISTANCE 2½ miles (4km)

TIME 1½ hours

PARKING Free at start

ROUTE FEATURES Mostly easy walking with just two stiles and a steep flight of steps. Some sections may be muddy. Please scoop the poop on the old railway and lead your dog through the donkey sanctuary; *dogs are not allowed into the owl and falconry centre*

Turn left out of the car park and walk down to the B3327 opposite The Worsley. Turn right past St John's Church, then right again up Castle Road. Just before the old railway bridge, turn left onto the footpath towards Shanklin and drop down past the industrial buildings onto the old railway line. Follow the track as it pulls away from the village, passes Yard Farm on your right, and runs through a shallow cutting.

A Now, look out for a gate and stile on your left; nip across, and walk down through the small field to a second stile and footpath signpost. Go over the stile and continue down a surfaced lane to the main road, taking care as you zigzag right and left across the road to join the bridleway towards Redhill Lane. The route continues through the Isle of Wight Donkey Sanctuary, leaving the site at a wooden five-bar gate.

PUBLIC TRANSPORT Regular bus service from all the main Island towns (01983 532373)

REFRESHMENTS The Worsley: Ushers beers, dining and family rooms
Aviary Café: hot and cold drinks/lunches

PUBLIC TOILETS Wroxall village centre and Appuldurcombe House

ORDNANCE SURVEY MAPS Explorer OL29 (Isle of Wight)

Park Hill Farm
Winstone Farm
81
Sewage Works
55
Yard Farm
Stenbury Trail
Redhill La.
Sandpit Copse
Freemantle Copse
Redhill Farm
54
Appuldurcombe Park
72
Worsley Trail
Gat Cliff
Appuldurcombe Farm
OWL AND FALCONRY CENTRE
Obelisk
Cemy
Appuldurcombe Down
Appuldurcombe House
80
Sch
3 P
Wroxall
Baycroft Farm
PO
1 KM
HALF MILE

What is the full dedication of St John's Church, Wroxall?

Cross the wooden footbridge, then bear right along the signposted bridleway GL36. The track winds through a small wooden gate, and emerges from a patch of trees to run along the right-hand side of an open field. There are good views of Appuldurcombe Down on the left,

This walk takes you through the heart of the **Isle of Wight Donkey Sanctuary**. From its small beginnings in 1987, the sanctuary moved to Lower Winstone Farm in 1994 and now provides a safe, permanent home for more than 200 donkeys. The sanctuary is always popular with children, so allow plenty of time for your visit – entry is free, but you might just be tempted to adopt a donkey while you're looking round.

before another small gate marks the start of a path that leads you out between hedges to Redhill Lane. Zigzag left and right across the lane and join bridleway GL49 towards Stenbury Down for the waymarked climb to a five-bar gate at Freemantle Copse.

B Turn left just beyond the gate, and follow the bridleway towards Wroxall through the imposing Freemantle Gate at the edge of the Appuldurcombe estate. A hundred yds (91m) farther on, bear right along the main gravelled track towards Appuldurcombe House and continue to the car park opposite the entrance to the owl and falconry centre.

Turn left at the car park and follow the drive as it leads away from Appuldurcombe House. Bear right onto Appuldurcombe Road, and continue to the main B3327. Go carefully as you zigzag right and left across the main road, then climb the steep wooden steps to rejoin the old railway. Turn right, and retrace your outward steps back to Wroxall village and the car park where your walk began. ●

Falconry is one of the world's oldest sports, and was a favourite with King Henry VIII when he visited **Appuldurcombe House** (see walk 17) in 1539. **The Isle of Wight Owl and Falconry Centre** at Appuldurcombe features flying displays with raptors from around the world, as well as aviaries containing owls, falcons, hawks, vultures and kites. There's an indoor flight barn for wet days, as well as a souvenir shop and Aviary Café.

St John's Church, Wroxall

Fort Victoria

START Fort Victoria Country Park
DISTANCE 2½miles (4km)
TIME 1½ hours
PARKING Free car park at the start
ROUTE FEATURES This walk mainly follows roughly-surfaced tracks. There are a handful of stiles, and the rural section may be muddy. *Please lead dogs near grazing animals, and scoop the poop in the country park*

Starting from Fort Victoria Country Park, the walk follows the coastal path to the outskirts of Yarmouth. After doubling back across grazing fields you'll rejoin the coastal path for the return to Fort Victoria, where there's a good range of facilities and family attractions.

🖊 Face the fort and walk around the left-hand end by the toilets. Turn left after 50 yds (46m), signposted towards the coastal path and nature trail, and climb up through the woods to the coastal path. Turn left along the roughly surfaced woodland track, passing the backs of some houses on your left. Bear right when you meet the access road to the fort, follow it for 100 yds (91m), then continue along the coastal path as it bears off to the left towards Yarmouth.

The path will lead you through a small patch of woodland before dropping down a couple of steps and turning right along the sea wall. Here you'll enjoy good views of St James' Church tower standing sentinel above the little town of Yarmouth and its attractive harbour. Bear right as you reach the information panel at Norton Spit Site of Special Scientific Interest, and continue to the main road at Halletts Shute.

Ⓐ Cross over and turn left along the pavement for 80 yds (73m). Now turn right down Gasworks Lane and follow the Freshwater Way until you reach a stile on your

PUBLIC TRANSPORT Bus services from all the main Island towns (01983 532373)
REFRESHMENTS Verdi's café bar: snacks, light lunches, hot meals, cream teas, ices, patio with superb coastal views
PUBLIC TOILETS At the start
ORDNANCE SURVEY MAPS Explorer OL29 (Isle of Wight)

right, just beyond Norlands Cottage. Nip across, and follow footpath F2 as it branches off towards Halletts Shute, following the hedge on your right-hand side. A second stile leads you along a narrow enclosed path to meet the main road, where you turn left along the pavement.

B Take the first turning on your right into Westhill Lane, signposted towards the Fort Victoria Country Park. Pass Braxton Meadow on your left, cross the little white-railed bridge, then turn left into Linstone Drive along footpath F3 towards Colwell. As the road bears

around to the right, go off to the left along a grassy lane and through a wooden kissing-gate into a long narrow field.

Fort Victoria was part of a chain of defences commissioned by Queen Victoria to protect the Solent against the French. The buildings were completed in 1855, but more powerful naval guns quickly rendered them obsolete and the fort was later converted into a submarine mining depot. You can see a short section of tramway from this period in the car park. The fort was originally triangular, but the large barrack blocks on the third side were demolished in 1969.

Where might you see marram grass, sea lavender and sea holly?

The Solent and Hurst Castle from the coastal path

Elder, dog-rose, blackthorn and gorse are your companions as you follow the right-hand hedge through an opening beside a stile into the next field. Here the path swings across to follow the left-hand hedge until an indistinct trackway crosses your path through a field gate on the left. Go over the stile in front of you, and continue along the right-hand side of the next field until you reach another stile.

C Cross the stile and turn right onto the signposted coastal path along Monks Lane until you reach the entrance to a distinctive row of bungalows at Cliff End. Just here, dodge away to your right and follow the coastal path as it winds between the fences around the edge of the housing estate. Soon the path turns right, shakes off

A woodland nature trail now follows part of the old military road that once linked Fort Victoria to Fort Albert – you can pick up a trail guide from the Ranger Base near the start of this walk. More formal attractions at the Fort include the **Island Planetarium** and a marine aquarium, as well as the **Sunken History** exhibition and a model railway.

the houses, and continues into the wooded country park. There are bench seats here and lovely views across the Solent towards Hurst Castle.

Drop down a flight of steps, and continue for 600 yds (549m) through the woods to a signposted fork in the track. Turn left here, towards the refreshments and toilets, for the short way back to the fort.

5 *Around Brighstone*

START Warnes Lane car park.
DISTANCE 2½ miles (4km)
TIME 1½ hours
PARKING Free parking at the start
ROUTE FEATURES This walk combines village and field edge paths with a bridleway route over high heathland. There are eight stiles, a fairly steep climb, and the route will be muddy in wet weather

The walk heads south past Brighstone Mill before picking its way across farmland to the church and on towards The Countryman. Now you'll climb steeply onto heathland in the hills behind the village, where you can look down on your route through the landscape below. An attractive bridleway leads you back to the village and its museum.

Leave the car park on footpath BS25 towards Galley Lane and follow it out to the Methodist Church. Bear left into Wilberforce Road, then zigzag right and left onto a signposted footpath. Cross the plank bridge, go through the kissing-gate, and follow the path as it winds beside an attractive brook and through a second kissing-gate to Brighstone Mill. Turn left onto Wicken Hill Lane and continue for 200 yds (183m) to a signposted footpath on your left.

The track off the Downs

PUBLIC TRANSPORT Buses from Ryde, Newport, Freshwater and Totland (01983 532373)
REFRESHMENTS Three Bishops: Free house (snacks/bar meals) The Countryman: Free house (home cooked food) Brighstone tearooms
PUBLIC TOILETS At the start
ORDNANCE SURVEY MAPS Explorer OL29 (Isle of Wight)

A Nip over the stile and follow the left-hand field edge. A further three stiles carry you behind the buildings at Waytes Court, where the path bears left. Carry on along the field edge, cross another stile and a wooden footbridge, and continue until you reach the main road near the church. Turn right along the main road for the short distance past Bakehouse Cottage to the junction with Broad Lane.

Cross the stile on the far side of the road and turn immediately right, following footpath BS21 along the field edge towards Thorncross and Yafford. Soon the path bears to the left; follow it as it dives briefly between two hedges, then continue as before with the hedge on your right-hand side. Dodge to the right as you reach the far corner of the field, nip over the stile, and follow the left-hand field edge until you reach a stile 275 yds (251m) farther on. Turn left over the stile and continue along the right-hand field edge until, just beyond a pair of wooden gates, you meet the main road beside the newly-established Brighstone Parish Cemetery.

Brighstone has links with **William Wilberforce**, the 19th-century philanthropist who was influential in ending the slave trade. His son, Samuel Wilberforce, was the Rector of Brighstone during the 1830s, and William Wilberforce was a familiar sight in the village in the last years of his life. The family name is perpetuated in Wilberforce Road and the Wilberforce Hall.

B Cross the road and turn left along the grass verge; then, immediately past The Countryman, turn right up the signposted 'Bridle road to the Downs'. The green track climbs between wire fences, then bears left through an attractive tunnel of wind-sculpted trees and climbs more steeply to a four-way wooden signpost.

C Turn left here, along bridleway BS34 towards Brighstone. Now the views make up for the climb, with a wide sweep from St Catherine's Hill almost to the Needles. Brighstone itself is laid out like a map at your feet and it's easy to pick out the way that you've walked. The sandy track drops through a sunken way fringed with bracken and gorse, then swings to the left and continues between tall

There's an attractive row of National Trust thatched cottages in **North Street**, containing the Post Office and National Trust shop, as well as a locally-run **village museum**. Here you can see typical domestic items from the nineteenth century in a cottage tableau that includes an early sewing machine, bread oven and 'pegged' rug. Other displays focus on farming, land management and the village school.

hedgerow trees back into the village. Cross straight over into North Street, pass the museum and National Trust shop, then zigzag across the main road into Warnes Lane for the last few yards back to your car. ●

When was Brighstone's Wilberforce Church hall built?

National Trust cottages, North Street

Brading and Nunwell

START High Street, just north of the church
DISTANCE 2½ miles (4km)
TIME 1½ hours
PARKING Pay and display car park at the start
ROUTE FEATURES Generally easy walking, though there are several stiles and the woods may be muddy. *Please lead dogs through Nunwell Farm, and through the grounds of Nunwell House*

Starting from the heart of the little town, the walk uses footpaths and bridleways to complete a circuit of the Nunwell estate. There's a mix of scenery, from field edge paths and woodland tracks to a parkland finale with good views of Nunwell House.

Turn left out of the car park, cross the High Street and continue for 75 yds (69m) beyond the church. Turn right into Cross Street, then right again at the end, up a surfaced path with houses on your right. A few paces before the path meets West Lane, turn left onto footpath B27 towards Brading Down, following the edge of an open field with hedgerow trees on your right.

? *How many exhibits are there in the Lilliput antique doll and toy musuem?*

A Cross the stile at the top corner of the field and turn immediately right. After a few more paces the path merges with a wider bridleway that sweeps in from your left; join it, and continue through the woods until you reach a three-way wooden signpost. The Nunwell oaks were used for shipbuilding in Tudor and Napoleonic times, as well as for construction timbers in local manor houses. These woods were badly damaged in the great storm of October 1987, but have been extensively replanted.

PUBLIC TRANSPORT Island Line trains (08457 484950) also buses from Ryde, Sandown, Shanklin and Ventnor (01983 532373)
REFRESHMENTS The Snooty Fox and the Bugle Inn, the Secret Garden tearooms, and Brothers' traditional fish and chip shop
PUBLIC TOILETS At the start
ORDNANCE SURVEY MAPS Explorer OL29 (Isle of Wight)

There's plenty to see in and around Brading. Your route passes St Mary's Church and the **Lilliput Toy Museum**, as well as the Isle of Wight Wax Works with its **Chamber of Horrors** and candle carving demonstrations. And, within half a mile, you could take in the elegant Georgian Morton Manor, Adgestone vineyard, and the magnificent remains of Brading Roman villa.

B Turn right here onto bridleway B59 towards Nunwell and Hardingshute. Follow the track as it swings left past a substantial lodge cottage, where the trail becomes a surfaced lane. Pass Nunwell Farm and continue for 150 yds (137m) to a stile on your right.

C Nip over the stile and follow the signposted footpath B23 across open pasture towards Brading. Cross a plank bridge and stile beneath a massive old oak tree, and bear gently left past a waymarked oak tree on the crest of a low hill until you reach a footpath signpost 200 yds (183m) farther on. There are good views of Nunwell House on this section, *but do please respect the owner's privacy and keep to the public footpath.* Continue over a stile, still following the signposted path towards Brading as it tracks a rough line of oak trees heading just to the left of the lodge cottage on West Lane.

Brading High Street

D The plank bridge and stile beside the cottage will lead you out onto West Lane. *There's no pavement here, so take care as you turn right* and continue for 80 yds (73m) beyond the entrance to Nunwell House. Turn right into Doctors Lane and retrace your outward steps back to the start. ●

Nunwell House

Nunwell House was the ancestral home of the influential Oglander family from 1522, and King Charles I spent his last night of freedom here during the Civil War. More recently, the **East Wight Home Guard** was based at Nunwell in World War II, and a small museum now commemorates this period. The house was bought by Colonel and Mrs Aylmer in 1982, and is open three days a week from late May to early September.

7 West High Down

START The Needles Pleasure Park, Alum Bay.
DISTANCE 2½ miles (4km)
TIME 1½ hours
PARKING Large car park at the start (charges vary)
ROUTE FEATURES The first half of this walk is one long, steady climb. *Take great care near unfenced cliffs, especially with children. Please lead dogs near grazing animals*

Starting from Alum Bay, the walk makes a complete circuit of West High Down, the dramatic chalk headland that culminates at the Needles. The walk itself takes just 1½ hours, but you could easily spend half a day exploring the Needles headland and its attractions, or link the route with Walk 11 for a full day out.

From the miniature lighthouse at the car park entrance, set off up the public footpath that follows the signposted road towards the Needles Old Battery and tearoom. Follow the road around to the right and continue for almost ½ mile (805m) as it climbs towards the Old Battery. All the way along this section you'll enjoy spectacular views of Alum Bay, the Solent and Hurst Castle.

Ⓐ Bear left at the coastal footpath sign, following the narrow chalk path that climbs steeply away from the road towards the old Coastguard Cottages. Just below the cottages, the coastal path doubles back at a stile and climbs to the crest of West High Down, opening up a stunning 360-degree panorama all the way from Dorset to St Catherine's Point. Bear left along the top of the ridge, heading just a few degrees to the left of Tennyson's Monument, a mile or so in front of you.

> **?** *What replaced the original Nodes Beacon?*

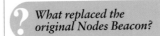

PUBLIC TRANSPORT Buses from all the main Island towns, also frequent open-top service from Yarmouth (01983 532373)
REFRESHMENTS Pleasure park: snacks, hot meals, licensed bar; Warren Farm (seasonal): sandwich lunches, farmhouse cream teas
PUBLIC TOILETS At the start
ORDNANCE SURVEY MAPS Explorer OL29 (Isle of Wight)

B Pass the small War Department marker stone on the summit, and follow the downland track as it drops down the ridge, still aiming slightly to the north of Tennyson's Monument. Clumps of gorse now dot the landscape as the track heads decisively towards the edge of the woods at the back of Tennyson Down. At the foot of the slope you'll come to a stile, right beside a wooden replica of the old Nodes beacon.

Until it was taken down in 1897, the Nodes Beacon was a well-known local landmark that still features on the seal of Totland Parish Council. The Rotary Club of

You'll either love the **Needles Pleasure Park**, or hate it. Besides the fairground rides and refreshments, there's the Alum Bay Glass Studio, the Isle of Wight Sweet Manufactory and, of course, the Alum Bay Sand Shop with chair lift rides to the beach. If the Pleasure Park isn't for you, try making a short diversion to the more dignified attractions of the National Trust's Needles Old Battery and tearoom.

West Wight erected this half-size replica beside a fragment of the original beacon to mark the Queen's Silver Jubilee in 1977.

C Just a few paces short of the stile, swing hard left onto footpath T25, signposted towards Alum Bay. The path drops gently down through the gorse bushes, passes a worked-out chalk pit and dives through a small thicket. Now there's a wire fence on your right-hand side and, in just under half a mile, you'll reach the gate to Warren Farm, nestling peacefully in the sequestered valley on your right. It's well worth dropping in here for a light lunch or traditional cream tea during the season when the farm is open. Beyond Warren Farm, simply follow the fence until you reach a stile straight in front of you. Nip across, drop down a dozen steps, and turn right onto the road to return to your car. ●

A small memorial at the Pleasure Park marks the spot where **Guglielmo Marconi** and his British associates established an experimental wireless telegraphy station in 1897. The station was based at the Needles Hotel, and Lord Kelvin made history here when he sent the first commercial radio telegram in June 1898. Eighteen months later, Marconi broadcast information to the United States liner *St Paul* for the first newspaper ever produced and printed at sea.

Alum Bay from the coastal path

Wootton Bridge

START Car park in Brannon Way (turning opposite Tesco Express)
DISTANCE 2¾ miles (4.4km)
TIME 1½ hours
PARKING Free car park at the start
ROUTE FEATURES This easy-going route includes six stiles. *Please lead dogs through the fields at Mousehill Farm, and take particular care at the railway crossings*

This delightful walk is a favourite with railway enthusiasts, and offers glimpses of Wootton station as it pushes out into lovely, unspoiled countryside. The route crosses the line twice before turning north through light woodland to reach the Old Mill Pond and Wootton Creek.

🥾 Turn right out of the car park, then left onto the main road opposite Tesco Express, and set off up the hill. Turn left into Station Road when you reach The Cedars, then take the second turning on the left into Packsfield Lane. A few houses line the route at first, but soon you'll find yourself treading an attractive lane between hedges of beech, holly, oak and bramble, with glimpses of Wootton Station away to the right. The well-surfaced path narrows and climbs gently past Packsfield Farmhouse to the gated railway crossing.

Wootton Creek

PUBLIC TRANSPORT Buses from Cowes, Newport and Ryde (01983 532373). Isle of Wight steam railway trains (01983 882204)
REFRESHMENTS The Sloop Inn (families welcome), The Cedars (play area)
PUBLIC TOILETS At the start
PICNIC/PLAY AREA Free picnic area at Wootton Station for railway users only
ORDNANCE SURVEY MAPS Explorer OL29 (Isle of Wight)

The Ryde and Newport Railway opened the line from Smallbrook Junction to Newport in 1875. The original platform at Wootton was west of Station Road, with an unusual booking office and waiting room built into an arch of the road bridge. Landslips led to the closure of this station in 1953 and, following preservation work, the Isle of Wight Steam Railway opened a new terminus on the present site in 1986.

A *Keep a good look out for trains as you cross the line* and fork left onto the narrow bridleway N7, signposted towards Littletown Lane. Zigzag right, then left, at Woodford Cottage and continue to the T-junction with bridleway N3.

Turn left towards Briddlesford Road, following the lane as it swings to the right in front of the white-painted 'Shiloh'.

B Pass Little Mousehill Farm Cottage and turn left over the stile along footpath N2, signposted towards Woodhouse Farm. Continue over three more stiles into a small wood, tracking the woodland edge until the path breaks clear at a waymarked stile. Bear gently right here along the side of the next field, go over the stile in the far corner, and turn left along bridleway N1 towards Wootton Bridge.

No 198 Royal Engineer *heads a train near Ashey*

? What is the penalty for trespassing on the railway?

Several of the woodlands south of Wootton Bridge are included within the **Briddlesford Copses Site of Special Scientific Interest**. This official designation puts them among England's finest wildlife locations, legally protected by English Nature. Beyond the second railway crossing the route passes through Hurst Copse, notable for hornbeam, alder and wild service trees, as well as dormice, red squirrels, and eight species of bats.

C Keep Woodhouse Farm to your right as you drop down and bear right to the railway crossing. *Watch out for trains as you cross the line once again*, then bear left and follow the lane as it winds its way north through a patchwork of woods and fields. Take the chance to explore the wildlife as you pass Hurst Copse on your right, or simply continue until you reach the pretty Fernhill Farm on your left-hand side. Here the lane becomes a surfaced drive as it runs close to the Old Mill Pond for the remaining short distance to the Sloop Inn.

D Turn left opposite the Sloop and follow the main road up through Wootton Bridge as far as Tesco Express on your right. Turn left into Brannon Way to return to your car.

●

9 Chale and Niton

START Chale village car park

DISTANCE 3½ miles (5.6km)

TIME 2 hours

PARKING Free car park at the start

ROUTE FEATURES *Take care with children and dogs on sections that follow the A3055. There are a handful of stiles and a long climb up onto St Catherine's Hill; some sections may be muddy*

A gentle stroll through Chale village leads you to a short section of the coastal path and the attractions at Blackgang Chine. Soon the walk cuts inland along a charming bridleway to Niton before climbing steadily over the flank of St Catherine's Down and dropping back into Chale.

Turn right out of the car park and walk down through the village past the Wight Mouse Inn to St Andrew's Church. Turn left onto the main road, then almost immediately right into The Terrace, signposted 'pedestrians to Blackgang'. Bear left at Brickhill Lodge onto the coastal path bridleway, an attractive tree-shaded path that opens up to give some sea views. Turn right as the coastal path rejoins the main road, and follow the wide left-hand grass verge past the Blackgang Chine roundabout.

Ⓐ Cross over here and continue for 200 yds (183m) to a stile in the hedge on your right. Nip over the stile and follow the signposted coastal path as it bears left around the edge of a grassy field to a second stile. Cross this one, too, and continue along the narrow path until a third stile leads you out onto the main road at the car park for St Catherine's Oratory. From here, a well-signposted 550 yd (503m) diversion will lead you up to the Oratory, and down again by the same route.

PUBLIC TRANSPORT Bus services from Ryde, Sandown, Shanklin, Ventnor and Yarmouth (01983 532373)

REFRESHMENTS Wight Mouse Inn, Chale. White Lion, Niton

PUBLIC TOILETS Niton village

ORDNANCE SURVEY MAPS Explorer OL29 (Isle of Wight)

Turn right through the car park to continue your walk. There's usually a refreshment caravan here, offering hot drinks and soup as well as a good selection of home-made cakes, biscuits and Chale Farm ice creams. Follow the coastal path up a short flight of steps as it leaves the car park and turns left along the clifftop. After 50 yds (46m) cross the stile on your left and head across the open field back to the main road. Turn right, and follow the wide grass verge for 100 yds (91m).

B Cross over the road, and turn left along bridleway NT52 towards Niton. After 100 yds (91m) the bridleway turns off to the right; this is fast, easy walking along a delightful grassy track with sweeping sea views. Simply follow the wire fence on your left until the track drops between hedges to rejoin the main road just west of Niton.

C Turn left along the grass verge and continue onto the pavement as it bears left through Niton village. Soon you'll reach the church of St John the Baptist on your left; turn left here to begin the climb up Pan Lane towards St Catherine's Down. Your way continues straight ahead onto bridleway NT53 as it follows Bury Lane through a tunnel of low trees, with glimpses of the Pepperpot on your left-hand side.

D At the T-junction with Crocker Lane you'll see Hoy's Monument sticking above the trees on the

St Andrew's Church, Chale

Two towers stand sentinel over St Catherine's Down. To the south, the 14th-century St Catherine's Oratory – known locally as the **Pepperpot** – is Britain's second oldest lighthouse. A mile (91m) farther north, Hoy's Monument commemorates a visit by Tsar Nicholas I in 1814.

Why is there a lychgate at Niton church?

skyline straight ahead. Turn left here, and follow this lovely green path as it leads you around the valley to a small metal gate. Beyond the gate the path climbs gently across the open down, with far-reaching views on your right.

E At the crest of the hill another glorious vista carries your eye all the way along the south coast of the island as far as Tennyson Down and the Needles. The path continues through a pair of metal field gates, then passes between two wooden gateposts and bears to the right down the side of St Catherine's Down.

Follow the lane as it goes through a metal field gate and bears steadily left, continuing as a narrow path across rough ground and heading directly towards Chale church tower. Now the path drops to a wicket gate and turns left along a track through Chale Farm. Turn right at the junction with Upper House Lane and follow it down to the B3399. Zigzag left and right across the road to return to your car.

Mottistone and the coast

10

This varied walk follows byways, field and forest paths as it climbs steadily up to the halfway point at Long Stone. After dropping back through the woods to Mottistone Manor with its attractive gardens, a brisk walk down Ridget Lane prepares you for the final stretch along the cliff top coastal path.

START Chilton Chine
DISTANCE 3¾ miles (6km)
TIME 2 hours
PARKING Small free car park at the start
ROUTE FEATURES This route climbs almost 350 ft (107m) from the coast to the Long Stone. There are seven stiles, and some sections may be muddy. *Please lead dogs through fields beyond Strawberry Lane*

Cross the road from the car park and follow footpath BS71 towards Chilton Green. Beyond the green-painted chalets the track bears right, then left, to Chilton Green. Fork left onto the road at Chilton Farm; then, 150 yds (137m) farther on, fork right onto the byway towards Pitt Place. The tree-shaded track bears left, then climbs steadily to the T-junction at Pitt Place.

A Turn right onto the road and continue for 220 yds (201m) to the house at Grammar's Hill; *take care here, as there's no pavement on this section*. Turn left just beyond the house onto the narrow footpath BS67 towards Grammar's Common, climb up through a low tunnel of trees, and cross the stile into a conifer plantation. At first the path follows the left-hand edge of the plantation, before bearing away to the right and climbing deeper into the woods. A hundred yards (91m) farther on, a wider track crosses your path at a lonely waymark post. Keep straight on here, and follow the path as it curves away up the hill to a broader level section that contours gently around to the right.

PUBLIC TRANSPORT Bus services from Ryde, Sandown, Shanklin, Ventnor and Yarmouth (01983 532373)
REFRESHMENTS Mottistone Manor tea garden; Isle of Wight Pearl coffee shop
PUBLIC TOILETS None
ORDNANCE SURVEY MAPS Explorer OL29 (Isle of Wight)

The Long Stone

Soon the path drops gently through an area of young conifers, bears to the left, and leaves the plantation at a stile. There are sea views here, as well as a bench seat that offers a welcome refreshment break. Beyond the stile, follow the bare track across an open field to a second stile that leads out onto Strawberry Lane.

More than 35,000 pieces of jewellery are on display at Isle of Wight **Pearl**, just across Chilton Chine from the start of this walk. There's an open workshop, a large showroom, and you can also see replicas of dresses worn by **Queen Elizabeth I** and **Diana, Princess of Wales**. The site is open all year and entrance is free.

🅑 Turn right along the lane, follow it for 100 yds (91m), then swing left onto footpath BS84 at a metal gate that leads into the National Trust's Mottistone estate. Continue through a wicket gate and across the grazing fields to the Long Stone. Curiously enough there are two stones here – all that remains of the 4,000-year-old Neolithic burial chamber that was one of the oldest man-made structures on the island.

Directly beside the Long Stone, turn left past a short waymark post and follow the narrow sunken path that drops down through a patch of gorse, bracken and young oak. Continue through a kissing-gate as a forest track crosses your route;

drop down a few rough steps, then bear right along the indistinct path that winds through the woodlands surrounding Mottistone Manor. Bear left when you reach a more confident sunken track and follow it down through the trees to the B3399.

C Turn left past the entrance to Mottistone Manor, then right into Church Lane. Continue past the church into Ridget Lane and follow

the lane as it bears left, leaves the tarmac behind, and heads straight for the coast. A stretch of fast, easy walking brings you to the Military Road; cross over, jump the stile opposite and join footpath BS75 for the final link with the coastal path.

> **?** *How often do they cut the grass in Mottistone churchyard?*

Fifty yards (46m) farther on, you'll come to a pair of stiles. *Stop here, and gather your thoughts, for hidden in the brambles between the two stiles there's a deep concrete sump that could easily break your leg.* Your way lies straight ahead, so *cross the stiles with care* and follow the wire fence on your right. Now you can smell the sea, and a final stile brings you, at last, to the coast path.

D Turn left, and follow the path along the top of these crumbling southern cliffs; *once again care is needed, as you're only a few feet from the edge on this section.* Now you can see the whitewashed buildings at Isle of Wight Pearl, just beyond Chilton Chine – and, to your left, you should be able to pick out most of the circular route that you've followed since leaving your car.

Just short of Isle of Wight Pearl, a set of steps leads down into the chine. Turn left here, for the short distance back to the car park. ●

> A **manor house** has stood at Mottistone since the time of Domesday, though the present buildings date from the 16th and 17th centuries. A landslide engulfed the rear of the property in 1703, and it wasn't until the 1920s that John Seely – later Lord Mottistone – had the earth carted away as part of an extensive renovation programme. Lord Mottistone bequeathed the house and its 650-acre (236ha) estate to the National Trust in 1963.

Mottistone Manor

Freshwater and Tennyson Down

START National Trust car park at the top of Highdown Lane
DISTANCE 3¾ miles (6km)
TIME 2 hours
ROUTE FEATURES The gradients on this walk are long and steady, rather than steep. *Please take particular care near unfenced cliff edges especially with children.* Dog should be led near grazing animals on the Down, and through Afton Marsh nature reserve

This varied route begins with dramatic coastal landscapes, then drops into Freshwater Bay for a change of scene. After continuing through Afton Marsh nature reserve, a woodland stroll along the back of the Downs completes the loop. For a longer walk, the route can easily be combined with Walk 7.

🖉 Set off as if to leave the car park by road, then turn immediately left past a low wooden barrier into the National Trust's Tennyson Down estate. Follow the lightly wooded green lane for nearly ½ mile (805m) until you reach a replica of the old Nodes Beacon standing prominently beside a stile at a footpath 'cross roads'.

🅐 Double back to your left at the beacon, now following the coastal footpath as it heads out through some gorse bushes towards the Tennyson Memorial on the summit of the Down. There are bench seats around the memorial, which is a natural focus for walkers. From here, a breathtaking panorama encompasses a wide sweep along the island's south coast from St Catherine's, as well as Hurst Castle, the Solent and the New Forest in the north. *But don't let any of that distract you from the fact that the memorial is scarcely 25 yds (23m) from the cliff edge, with a 160-ft (49m) drop to the beach below.*

🅑 Continue along the scant downland path past the memorial

PUBLIC TRANSPORT Open-top bus service from Yarmouth and Freshwater to the High Down Inn, at the bottom of Highdown Lane (01983 532373)
REFRESHMENTS Freshwater Bay Tea Rooms; Albion Hotel; Fat Cat bar
PUBLIC TOILETS Gate Lane, Freshwater Bay
ORDNANCE SURVEY MAPS Explorer OL29 (Isle of Wight)

Freshwater Bay

towards Freshwater Bay, keeping about 50 yds (46m) from the cliff edge. There's an information panel near the kissing-gate where you leave the Down, and soon you'll join the surfaced path that winds down above Watcombe Bay and bears left through another kissing-gate onto a small lane. Follow the signposted coastal path along the lane, past Freshwater Bay House holiday centre, until you reach the junction with Gate Lane.

Ⓒ Turn right at the end, towards the beach; then, after 100 yds (91m), turn left at the tearooms into Coastguard Lane. Pass the Fat Cat bar and continue as the gravelled road merges into a country path and goes through a

waymarked kissing-gate into Afton Marsh local nature reserve. Here, a second kissing-gate leads down six steps and across a boardwalk to a fork in the path; keep left, and continue out onto Blackbridge Road. *There's no pavement on this section, so do watch out for the occasional car as you turn left along the road* as far as the T-junction opposite St Agnes' Church.

This charming little building is the only thatched church on the island and looks much older than it really is. Much of the building material was recovered from a derelict old farmhouse, and a large stone near the vestry door carries the date 1694. Yet, despite this, the church was actually built in 1908 to replace the former mission church or 'iron room' that stood nearby. The land was given by the Tennyson family.

In addition to Tennyson Down, the National Trust now owns much of the **West Wight** peninsula, including West High Down and Headon Warren. The area is part of the chalk ridge that forms the island's backbone – and once linked the island to Ballard Down near Swanage in Dorset. The natural woodland was cleared for grazing during the Stone Age, and the Downs now contain some of Britain's finest chalk grassland.

D Zigzag left and right across the main road and continue through a kissing-gate up footpath F46 towards Tennyson Down and the Needles. The path runs between hedges to a waymarked wicket gate, then follows the edge of an open field beside the hedge on your right-hand side. After 200 yds (183m), a signpost points your way to the right, through a field gate onto a delightful tree-shaded green lane. Simply follow the path past a National Trust marker stone until you reach a fork 100 yds (91m) beyond the worked-out quarry on your left. Keep left here, through the low tunnel of trees that leads you to a kissing-gate and a small grassy clearing, where you drop down into the car park where your walk began. ●

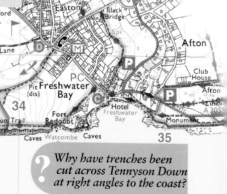

? *Why have trenches been cut across Tennyson Down at right angles to the coast?*

85

12 Newchurch

START School Lane car park

DISTANCE 4 miles (6.4km)

TIME 2 hours

PARKING Free at start

ROUTE FEATURES Generally easy walking, with only a few stiles, though the woodland sections may be muddy. Please lead dogs through the churchyard and along the short sections of road, as well as on the Bembridge Trail and through the newly-planted woodland

The walk drops steeply downhill from Newchurch and turns briefly east along the old railway, now part of the national cycle network. From here it turns north to follow the Bembridge Trail between Knighton and Kern Farm, before dropping down into Alverstone village. A final section along the old railway and Newchurch Parish Nature Trail completes the loop.

Turn right out of the car park, then right again past the Pointer Inn. Dodge to your right through the church gates and continue to a small iron gate at the corner of the churchyard. Follow the narrow stepped path steeply downhill, and turn left at the bottom onto a tree-shaded lane. Rejoin the road, turn right, and follow it to Newchurch Crossing. *Take care here, as there's no pavement and the road is quite narrow.*

A Turn right onto the old railway, now part of the Sustrans national cycle network. After 550 yds (503m) turn left onto bridleway NC53 towards Knighton, a pleasant dirt track with good downland views. Continue onto Lower Knighton Lane, and keep straight on at the next junction towards Newport and Ryde. Pass Knighton Farm, where the Bembridge Trail swings in from the left, and keep going until the road bears gently left.

PUBLIC TRANSPORT Limited bus service from Newport and Sandown (01983 532373)

REFRESHMENTS Pointer Inn: Gales ales, home-made food, family garden

PUBLIC TOILETS None

PICNIC/PLAY AREA None, but opportunities for informal picnics along the route

ORDNANCE SURVEY MAPS Explorer OL29 (Isle of Wight)

B Turn right here onto bridleway NC45 towards Knighton waterworks and Alverstone. The lane winds through a small group of cottages, then climbs gently through light mixed woodland until a couple of blue waymarks at Harts Ash Farm point your way to the right. Now the trail drops through a tree-shaded sunken way; bear left at the end of this hollow, signposted towards Kern. The sandy track winds onwards, crosses the access road to Knighton sandpit, and comes to a four-way signpost at a byway crossroads.

Continue through the field gate straight ahead, following the Bembridge Trail towards Kern and Alverstone. The grassy track bears to the left beside open fields, with a hedge on your left and wide views to the right. Another gate leads you through a short section shaded by trees and high gorse, until the path climbs gently from a third gate to the buildings at Kern Farm.

C Double back to your right through the farm gate, following the bridleway towards Alverstone as it swings left onto a small

What does the name 'Alverstone' mean?

All Saints, Newchurch

country lane. Stick with the lane as it swings back to the right and drops gently down to the beautifully renovated buildings at Chiddle's Farm. Nip over the stile ahead of you and continue along the right-hand field edge, following the footpath towards Alverstone and Knighton. Continue over the stile in the far corner of the field until, after 70 yds (64m), the path turns left into Alverstone. Turn right through the village as far as the old railway crossing with its white painted gates, where the old station house still stands beside the national cycleway.

🅓 Turn right along the cycleway and follow it to a four-way signpost 450 yds (411m) farther on. Turn left here over a little footbridge onto footpath NC11 towards

Newchurch, continuing through a kissing-gate and a narrow belt of trees. Cross an open field to a second kissing-gate, then fork right through the woodland and across an area of open heath and bracken. Continue until the woods close in again and you reach an unsign-posted turning on your right. Turn here, cross the waymarked stile and small plank bridge, and climb gently up through a newly planted woodland. Bear left at the top, following the waymarked route along the top of the plantation.

As the path approaches Newchurch it runs beside All Saints graveyard wall; keep the wall on your left, then go through an opening and up three steps into the field behind the church. Turn right along the tarmac path, then left at the end to retrace your steps past the Pointer and back to the car park. ●

The 11-mile **Bembridge Trail** is one of eight inland routes linking the interior of the island with the coastal path. Starting from Shide on the outskirts of Newport, the trail threads its way through woods and downland scenery to Nunwell House and the historic town of Brading (see Walk 6). The route continues past Bembridge windmill (Walk 15) to reach the mouth of the River Yar at Bembridge.

Carisbrooke and its castle

There are plenty of castle views along this route, which pushes out to the west of Carisbrooke along farm tracks and quiet green lanes. A steep climb brings you up to the Tennyson Trail, and the walk loops back through Carisbrooke village before closing with a dramatic final section around the castle ramparts.

START Carisbrooke Priory car park

DISTANCE 4¼ miles (6.8km)

TIME 2 hours

PARKING Free parking at the start

ROUTE FEATURES *Please lead your dog through the farms and along White Lane, as well as in Carisbrooke village*

Face the castle, turn left along the wide grass verge, and fork right into Froglands Lane. The road bears away to the right at the bottom of the hill, but your way lies straight ahead along the footpath that follows the gravelled track towards Froglands Farm. Pass the picturesque farm buildings on your left and follow the tree-shaded track as it bears right past a bridleway signpost and pulls out into open countryside. There are glorious views of Bowcombe Down on your right here, before the path bears to the right and drops down an old sunken way through a tunnel of trees. Pass the junction with footpath N104, and continue for 170 yds (155m) to a fork in the path.

Ⓐ Turn left here onto an attractive green lane that runs between hedges to a T-junction at Bowcombe Farm. Turn right, and follow the byway as it winds past the farm buildings and climbs gently up to the busy Bowcombe Road. Cross over, turn right, and follow the pavement for 250 yds (229m) before turning left onto bridleway N127 towards White Lane and the Tennyson Trail. The tree-shaded

PUBLIC TRANSPORT Bus connections from all the main Island towns (01983 532373)

REFRESHMENTS The Eight Bells: Free house, all day menu, families welcome, non-smoking dining area, garden and play area; The Waverley: Free house, bar food, garden

PUBLIC TOILETS Carisbrooke High Street

ORDNANCE SURVEY MAPS Explorer OL29 (Isle of Wight)

Carisbrooke Castle ramparts

track climbs steeply to a metal field gate and, a few paces farther on, you'll reach a crossroads with the Tennyson Trail. It's a good place to stop for a breather, as well as to admire the view across the valley towards Garstons Down.

Ⓑ Turn right onto the Tennyson Trail, and follow the rough farm road that leads you down into Carisbrooke village. Much of this section is hemmed in by trees, but there are occasional views of the castle to your right and, in late summer, a profusion of butterflies will keep you company on the road. The trail drops gently at first, then more steeply as you approach the outskirts of Carisbrooke and reach the junction with a quiet residential road. Turn left, then bear right into High Street; cross

over, and follow the pavement on the left-hand side of the road. Pass The Waverley, keep straight on at the mini-roundabout, and continue through St Mary's churchyard to the south door of this imposing church.

Ⓒ Drop down the steps immediately opposite the church, cross the road, and turn into Castle Street. Continue along the charming causeway beside the Lukely Brook; then, 50 yds (46m) farther on, swing left up Castle Lane and follow it to the junction with the castle access road. Cross over, take the footpath directly ahead of you, and follow it as it skulks through the trees at the foot of the castle mound. Turn right after 25 yds (23m) up a flight of slippery stone steps, then bear left up a second flight that leads you up onto the castle ramparts.

Bear left, and continue along the ramparts with the castle walls on your right. Follow the walls around a sharp right-hand bend; then, just before the next bend, turn sharp left onto the waymarked footpath that leads steeply down off the castle mound. At the foot of the slope the narrow path bears right and runs across the little valley to meet your outward route at Froglands Lane. Turn left, and retrace your outward steps for the short way back to your car.

Who was Rev William James Stobart?

Carisbrooke Castle stands in a commanding position close to the centre of the island, and the site was probably fortified in both Roman and Saxon times. The present castle was founded by the Normans, and development continued right through to the Tudor period. Later, King Charles I was held prisoner at Carisbrooke during the Civil War – but nowadays, children are more likely to be fascinated by the donkeys that power the **giant waterwheel** beside the castle's well.

14 *The western Yar*

START River Road car park
DISTANCE 3¾ miles (6km)
TIME 2 hours
PARKING Pay-and-display car park at the start
ROUTE FEATURES Active wheelchair users can enjoy the nicely-surfaced outward route along the old Freshwater railway line. The return loop includes eight stiles, and follows well-signposted rural paths that may be muddy

There are great river views as the walk strikes out down the old railway path along the eastern shore of the River Yar. After crossing the causeway and climbing to the picturesque Red Lion beside All Saints' Church, the return journey along country paths is largely out of sight of the river.

Turn right out of the main car park entrance, pass the primary school, and turn right into Mill Road. As the road turns left into Station Road, continue along the signposted footpath towards Freshwater and Broad Lane. Bear right along the edge of the river, and through a wicket gate onto the old railway path towards The Causeway and Freshwater.

Ⓐ This well-engineered route will carry you all the way south to The Causeway.

Ⓑ Footpath F24 branches off towards Wilmingham Lane as you reach Backet's Plantation. Then, as the old line approaches The Causeway, a bench seat near the old landing stage makes a good spot to stop for a few minutes to watch the birds, or simply to enjoy the river views.

Ⓒ Turn right over The Causeway, pass the wartime pill-box on your left, and climb the short hill to the church and the Red Lion pub. Directly in front of the church turn right onto the Freshwater Way,

PUBLIC TRANSPORT Bus services from all the main Island towns (01983 532373). Wightlink ferry service from Lymington (0870 582 7744)
REFRESHMENTS The Red Lion, Freshwater. Yarmouth: Good selection of cafés and pubs
PUBLIC TOILETS Bridge Road, Yarmouth.
ORDNANCE SURVEY MAPS Explorer OL29 (Isle of Wight)

The Yar valley has been settled since prehistoric times and contains several important **archaeological sites**. The medieval town of Yarmouth was listed as Eremue in Domesday Book and the castle, completed in 1547, was garrisoned during the Civil War. A small ferry carried travellers across the estuary until the old Yar bridge was built in 1863; it was replaced by the present bridge in 1987.

which will carry you all the way back to Yarmouth. The narrow path runs beside the churchyard to a stile, then continues briefly between wire fences with fields on each side.

A second stile leads you out onto a tarmac lane; keep straight on here, with a row of bungalows on your left and views to the river on your right. The lane continues to a fork at Kings Manor Farm. Follow the Freshwater Way as it dodges to the left over a smart double stile and plank bridge and bears to the right along a well-

signposted route behind the farm buildings. Cross the next stile, too, and continue through a small plantation.

> **?** When did Isle of Wight Council attain the national rights-of-way target?

Wightlink ferry Cenwulf *leaving Yarmouth*

Beyond this little wood, the path bears left through a kissing-gate and leads you along a muddy farm track that climbs gently over a low summit with views across the river towards Yarmouth on your right. Continue through a small oakwood as the Freshwater Way veers to the right and carries you across two sets of stiles and plank bridges in quick succession.

Bear left here, climbing beside the woodland edge until the signposted path strikes out beside a wire fence separating two fields. Go over the stile at the top of another low hill and follow the muddy path as it winds through Saltern Wood to meet Gasworks Lane at a wooden barrier. Turn left onto the gravel road and continue past a couple of houses to the junction with the main A3054.

D Turn right, following the roadside pavement over the harbour bridge and past the Yarmouth Sailing Club to the mini-roundabout. Now, simply bear right to return to your car. ●

Bizarrely, the Isle of Wight boasts **two rivers with the same name.** This walk circles the estuary of the western Yar, while its more easterly namesake rises in Niton and flows towards the sea at Bembridge. The western Yar lies in an official area of outstanding natural beauty, and a raft of international designations protect its varied wildlife habitats. The estuary is especially rich in birdlife, and you may see curlew, little egret, or dark-bellied Brent geese.

Around Bembridge

15

This route encircles the little town of Bembridge. Starting from the lifeboat station, the walk cuts behind the Bembridge Coast Hotel to emerge on the cliff path. There are good views across Whitecliff Bay here, before turning inland through the woods to Bembridge windmill. The walk finishes with a bracing stretch along the beach.

START Lane End car park
DISTANCE 4¼ miles (6.8km)
TIME 2 hours
PARKING Pay-and-display car park at the start
ROUTE FEATURES Generally easy walking, *but do take care where the path runs close to the clifftops.* The final stretch along the beach may be impassable at high tide, but there's an alternative inland route

Face the sea and turn right along the coastal path B42, continuing as it turns right at the end of the small green. Cross the road at the Bembridge Coast Hotel and continue straight down the narrow footpath. Turn left at the end, following the coast path along Foreland Farm Lane. Turn right at the end into Howgate Road, then left into Beachfield Road, and continue along the coastal path as it bears right past the Coastguard Station and the Crab and Lobster pub.

Beyond Whitecliff Bay, the **Yarborough memorial** stands out clearly on the top of Culver Down. It was erected by public subscription in memory of Charles Anderson Pelham, Earl of Yarborough, whose 'benevolence and kindness of heart endeared him to all who knew him'. The Earl, who lived at Appuldurcombe House near Wroxall (see Walks 3 and 17), was a keen sailor and first Commodore of the Royal Yacht Squadron. He died aboard his yacht *Kestrel* in September 1846.

Ⓐ Now the narrow path winds along the top of the crumbling

PUBLIC TRANSPORT Buses from Ryde, also limited service from Sandown (01983 532373)
REFRESHMENTS Crab and Lobster, Pilot Boat Inn, Toll Gate café, Lifeboat View café
PUBLIC TOILETS At the start, also opposite the Pilot Boat Inn. (No toilets at Bembridge windmill)
ORDNANCE SURVEY MAPS Explorer OL29 (Isle of Wight)

cliffs, with glorious views across Whitecliff Bay. At length, you reach the red brick buildings of the Bembridge Environmental Field Study Centre.

B Turn right here, following the signposted footpath past the study centre and up the woodland track to the junction with Hillway Road. Turn left, walk down the hill for 100 yds (91m), then turn right along the signposted footpath BB22

to Steyne Wood and Bembridge windmill. Two stiles punctuate the woodland route as the path crosses Sandown Road. Then, 100 yds (91m) farther on, bear right onto the attractive bridleway that climbs steadily to Bembridge windmill.

C Continue past the mill and keep straight on at the road junction. *Take care here, because there's no pavement for most of the next 500 yds (457m).* Two hundred yards (183m) beyond Grange Gardens, turn left onto footpath BB3, signposted towards The Point. The path drops into the woods, then swings to

Who gave Bembridge windmill to the National Trust?

Whitecliff Bay

the right and follows a wooden boardwalk to reach the gravelled lane leading to the Pilot Boat Inn. (*From here, the Toll Gate Café is just around the corner on your left*). Cross the road from the pub, and follow the right-hand public footpath up a private road until you reach a broad gravelled track.

Ⓓ Here, you have a choice of routes. Turn left, then right at the end of the track, to follow the signposted coastal footpath BB6. You'll find that the path along the low cliffs has been closed after about 100 yds (91m), but it's easy enough to drop down onto the beach for the remaining ½ mile (805m) back to the lifeboat station. With wide views across the Solent,

this is the nicer route – but it's heavy going along the shingle and you'll have to jump over low sea defences, too. Any reasonably fit adult should have no difficulty but, *at high tide or with young children, the alternative inland route makes a wiser choice*:

Cross the gravelled track and continue until the path meets Love Lane at a sharp bend. Zigzag left and right onto the road, and follow it until it merges with bridleway BB35. Keep straight along the bridleway as it crosses Swains Road and continue along Swains Lane to the junction with Lane End Road. Turn left here, for the last 300 yds (273m) back to the lifeboat station. ●

16 *Beside the Medina*

START Red Funnel ferry terminal, Cowes

DISTANCE 4½ miles (7.2km)

TIME 2½ hours

PARKING Cowes: Denmark Road pay-and-display car park, 75 yds (69m) from bus station

ROUTE FEATURES The surface of this old railway cycle route is ideal for more adventurous wheelchair users. Fouling by dogs is an offence

This level walk leaves Cowes along residential roads and joins the old railway cycle path on the edge of town. There are plenty of river views and, in a couple of places, you can walk right down to the water's edge. After crossing Dodnor Creek nature reserve the walk enters Newport through an industrial estate on the old station site.

Leave the ferry terminal under the arch and turn left into High Street. Pass the Carvel Lane bus station just off High Street on your right and bear left into the pedestrianised area. Continue into Shooters Hill and bear left at the top into Birmingham Road, signposted towards the floating bridge. Zigzag right and left at the Duke of York into York Street and keep going over the staggered crossroads into Pelham Road. Take the first turning right into South Road, climb the short hill, and turn

Royal Yacht Squadron, Cowes

PUBLIC TRANSPORT High-speed ferry service from Southampton (0870 444 8898). A frequent bus service links Newport with Cowes (01983 532373)

REFRESHMENTS You'll be spoilt for choice in Newport and Cowes, but there are no refreshment facilities in between the two towns

PUBLIC TOILETS Cowes: Denmark Road; Newport: South Street (next to bus station)

ORDNANCE SURVEY MAPS Explorer OL29 (Isle of Wight)

left at the top into Arctic Road. Continue past the UK Sailing Academy until, at the very end of the road, you zigzag right and left onto the signposted cycle path towards Newport.

Ⓐ The path edges its way clear of industrial Cowes through a tunnel of oak, ash and birch. Just beyond the chimneys of Cowes power station on the far bank, look out for attractive views down the small creek on your left. So far there's been little to betray the path's railway ancestry but, a short way past the signposted footpath CS33 to Northwood on your right, you'll come to the broken remains of an iron and timber bridge, with trees growing up through the old road decking.

Ⓑ There are more glimpses of colourful moored sailing craft and, half hidden in the trees on the far bank, look out for the Victorian pinnacles of St Mildred's Church in Whippingham. The original church was extravagantly rebuilt in the mid-19th century, and used by the Royal family during their stays at nearby Osborne House. The views

> **?** *What's the name of the derelict old paddle-steamer halfway along the far bank? (You'll need your binoculars for this one)*

Crossing Dodnor Creek nature reserve

gradually open out around Pinkmead, and soon you'll spot the old paddle-steamer slowly rusting away near the marina on the far bank.

C Cross Stag Lane, and the trestle viaduct across Dodnor Creek nature reserve. The path now climbs to a level crossing with Dodnor Lane, in place of the bridge that originally carried the road above the railway. A little farther on, modern industrial buildings begin to huddle round on the northern outskirts of Newport. Look out, here, for the huge rolling gantry and trackways crossing the path from NEG Micon, one of the world's leading manufacturers of wind turbine blades. The facility is used to load their products onto barges for export around the world, and was specially designed to minimise the impact on the wild birds that feed on the adjacent mudflats.

This walk makes a great day out from **Southampton** using the Red Jet ferry. You'll have plenty of time to explore Cowes and Newport, and there's a bus every 15 minutes (half-hourly on Sundays) to get you back to the start. If you're already on the island, you might prefer to park in Newport and catch the bus to the start – that way, your car will be waiting for you at the end.

Dodnor Creek was dammed in the 1790s to power a proposed tide mill. Now a local **nature reserve**, the creek is rich in birdlife and you might see reed and sedge warblers as well as coot, moorhen and swans from the nearby bird hide. (Ring 01983 522195 to arrange for a key). The reserve stretches up towards the ancient woodlands of Dickson's Copse, where unusual butterflies flutter above the bluebells, primroses and orchids in the clearings.

D Now you're almost at the white painted gates that mark the end of the cycle path. Keep straight on at the Vectis Transport roundabout, and continue through the industrial estate to the A3020 bridge. *Take special care at this busy junction as you cross to the right-hand side, walk under the bridge and bear left across Hunnycross Way.* Almost at once, bear right at the mini-roundabout and head on up Hollyrood Street past the Railway Medina pub towards St Thomas's Church tower in the centre of town. Cross High Street, and continue through St Thomas Square into Pyle Street, where the car park is just a few yards away on your right. *Alternatively, keep straight on down Town Lane to reach the bus station in South Street.* ●

17 Godshill and Appuldurcombe

START The Old Smithy, Godshill

DISTANCE 5 miles (8km)

TIME 2½ hours

PARKING Free car park at the start

ROUTE FEATURES This strenuous walk climbs 600 ft (183m) to Stenbury Down. There are a handful of stiles, and the route may be muddy. *Please lead dogs through Godshill village, and near grazing animals*

After threading its way through Godshill village the walk heads south over the Worsley Trail to Gat Cliff. From here, it's an unremitting climb to the radio station high on Stenbury Down, where the route veers north and drops back down into rural farmland. The return leg makes its way back to Godshill past the brooding remains of Appuldurcombe House.

Turn right out of the car park, walk up the High Street, and continue around the right-hand bend to the Post Office. Cross over, turn left, and walk up Church Hollow towards the church. At the top of the hill you'll find the classic chocolate-box view of All Saints church tower rising above the thatched cottages on your right.

Ⓐ Turn left here and follow the lane south. Pass a junction on your left and then, 100 yds (91m) farther on, fork left into Sheepwash Lane. Continue past Sainham Farm to an unsignposted gap in the left-hand hedge, almost at the brow of the hill.

The influential Worsley family lived at **Appuldurcombe House** for three centuries. James Worsley had been a page to Henry VII; he was later knighted by Henry VIII and awarded a plethora of civil and military posts on the island. The family were shrewd political operators, married well, and successive generations continued to find Royal favour. They filled Appuldurcombe with pictures and important classical antiquities, but the collection was largely dispersed after the house was sold in 1855.

PUBLIC TRANSPORT Bus services from Newport, Sandown, Shanklin and Ventnor

REFRESHMENTS Tea gardens in Godshill village; The Griffin and The Cask & Taverners; Aviary café, Appuldurcombe

PUBLIC TOILETS At the start, and at Appuldurcombe House

ORDNANCE SURVEY MAPS Explorer OL29 (Isle of Wight)

B Turn hard left through the gap, and follow the path between newly planted saplings towards the left-hand corner of the woods ahead. Bear right along the woodland edge path and continue through the gates behind Sainham Farm to a stile on your right. Bear right over the stile onto footpath GL58, following the Worsley Trail towards Stenbury Down. The well-made track climbs to a mobile phone mast on your left, continues through a large steel gate, and bears right for the climb towards Gat Cliff. Soon a stile carries you through a patch of woodland to a second stile and a parting of the ways.

C Turn hard right here, and follow bridleway GL49 through a large metal gate towards Stenbury Down and Ventnor. Now a series of small gates leads you along the edge of an open field, past a turning on the right, and up the lightly wooded hill. Continue as the path swings to the left around the back of a disused chalk pit, and follow the hedge on your left-hand side towards the far radio station on Stenbury Down.

There are splendid views all along this section, and you can take in St Catherine's Oratory, Hoy's Monument and the south coast in one sweeping panorama. As you approach the transmitter, look out for a small metal gate on your left. Dodge through here, and join bridleway GL51 as it tracks the service road towards the mast, signposted to Week Down and Ventnor.

Appuldurcombe House

How close can you park to the radio station on Stenbury Down?

D Beyond the radio station, follow the service road as it sweeps around to the left and plunges down to meet Rew Lane opposite Bumble's Cottage.

E Turn left here; then, as the road veers to the right, keep straight on past Span Lodge along footpath GL47 towards Appuldurcombe House. Cross the stile and continue through the fields to Appuldurcombe, where a second stile leads you along the iron boundary railings with excellent views of the house.

Sir Robert Worsley began building the present house in 1701 on the site of an earlier Tudor mansion, but the project was a constant financial drain and was still unfinished when he died. His successor, Sir James Worsley, showed no interest in the house and it was left to his grandson, Sir Richard Worsley, to complete the

> **Godshill** village is a piece of Olde England wrapped up in pretty paper and sold back to you – but, for all that, the place is still worth a visit. Attractions like the cider barn, the toy museum and the model village all vie for your attention on the High Street, while **one of England's most photographed views** lies tucked away at the top of Church Hollow. Cream teas are mandatory.

building in the late 18th century. Sir Richard chose Capability Brown to landscape the park, and employed Thomas Chippendale to produce his furniture.

Further improvements were made to Appuldurcombe in the early 19th century before the Worsleys sold the estate in 1855. The new owner had planned to convert the house into a hotel, but the project came to nothing and Appuldurcombe was used for a time as a boys' school. The building later became a temporary refuge for French Benedictine monks, but from 1909 it lay empty. Its slow decline was hastened by damage during the Second World War, and by the 1950s the derelict house narrowly escaped demolition. Now in the care of English Heritage, the partly restored building is an alluring blend of stately home and ruined shell. Simply follow the

railings and stone wall around to the left, until you reach the car park at the entrance to Appuldurcombe House and the Isle of Wight Owl and Falconry Centre (see Walk 3).

F Zigzag left and right past the car park, and join footpath GL47 towards Godshill. Continue northwards to the imposing Freemantle Gate at the edge of the park.

G Go through the gate and keep straight on along bridleway GL44. From here it's plain sailing past Godshill Park House, where the track becomes a surfaced lane, all the way to the junction with Shanklin Road at Tyne Cottage. Turn left here, cross over the road, and follow the pavement back to the car park where your walk began. ●

Godshill

18 Newtown Harbour and Hamstead Point

START Horse & Groom pub, Ningwood
DISTANCE 5 miles (8km)
TIME 2½ hours
PARKING Please use the free public car park next to the pub
ROUTE FEATURES Much of this remote route follows wide gravelled tracks, but you'll also walk close to the water's edge and across low wooden causeways that may be submerged at high tide. The walk includes 10 stiles

This figure-of-eight route follows the coastal path and the Hamstead Trail as it sets out through a wooded area of scattered housing towards the Newtown River. Then, you'll traverse marsh and wetland habitats before rounding Hamstead Point and heading back along gravelled tracks through a rural mosaic of open fields and mixed woodland.

🐾 Turn left out of the car park, follow the narrow verge beside the main road for 200 yds (183m) to Hamstead Drive, and turn left again up the signposted coastal path towards Hamstead. Follow the gently curving gravel road as it heads north past scattered houses and into Nunneys Wood. Cross the bridge at Ningwood Lake, and climb gently through the woods to a fork ⬤ in the road at Pigeon Coo Farm. Keep straight on along the coastal path and Hamstead Trail to a

second fork, 200 yds (183m) farther on.

🅐 Fork right onto footpath S28 towards Yarmouth, still following the gravel road through mixed oak and conifer woodland. Gradually the trees slip behind you, and the road continues between hedges with occasional glimpses of the Newtown River up ahead. This is easy walking, but there are landmarks along the way; footpath S5 turns off to your left, and you pass

PUBLIC TRANSPORT Buses from Yarmouth and Newport (01983 532373)
REFRESHMENTS Horse & Groom, Ningwood: Good range of bar snacks and meals, no smoking area, garden and play area
PUBLIC TOILETS None
ORDNANCE SURVEY MAPS Explorer OL29 (Isle of Wight)

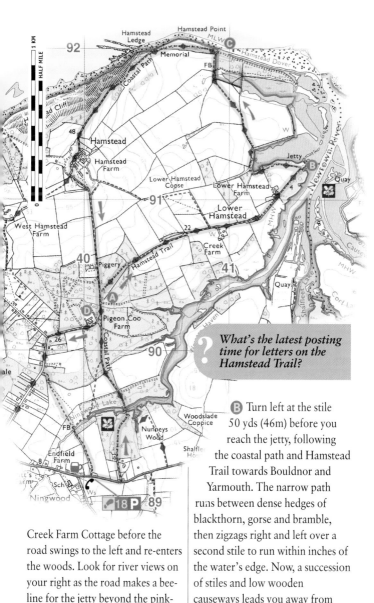

What's the latest posting time for letters on the Hamstead Trail?

Creek Farm Cottage before the road swings to the left and re-enters the woods. Look for river views on your right as the road makes a bee-line for the jetty beyond the pink-washed Lower Hamstead Farm.

B Turn left at the stile 50 yds (46m) before you reach the jetty, following the coastal path and Hamstead Trail towards Bouldnor and Yarmouth. The narrow path runs between dense hedges of blackthorn, gorse and bramble, then zigzags right and left over a second stile to run within inches of the water's edge. Now, a succession of stiles and low wooden causeways leads you away from the river and out into farmland.

It's hard to overstate the quiet charm of the **Newtown River**. The long, narrow creeks which thread their way between low wooded hills are a favourite haunt for yachtsmen, while the extensive mudflats provide rich feeding grounds for wading birds and other wildfowl. The National Trust bought the estuary in 1965 after local people campaigned against a proposed nuclear power station at Hamstead. The whole area is also officially protected for its outstanding landscape and wildlife.

Continue along the left-hand edge of the field as it rises beside the hedgerow trees on your left to give river views on the right-hand side. Just beyond the crest of this gentle rise, the path turns half left over a stile and heads diagonally across an open field. Nip over the stile in the far corner, and cross the long wooden causeway over a shallow arm of the Newtown River. From here, the path leads between thick hedges towards the sound of the surf on Hamstead Point.

C Now the coastal path lives up to its name as it drops down a dozen steps and swings to the left along a grassy track right next to the beach. As you round Hamstead Point, look out for the little stone memorial tucked in the bushes on your left; then, follow the coast path as it cuts inland up a stony, tree-shaded track that levels off and opens out with a field on the left-hand side. This is pleasant, gently rolling farmland with old trees in the hedgerows, but spare a backward glance for the seascape behind you.

Ningwood Lake

There's a final glimpse across the Solent to Lymington as the coastal path bears left, then right, over the signposted stile at Hamstead Farm. Follow the gravel road as it winds past Grange Cottage and continues as footpath S30 towards the Newport/Yarmouth road. The road bears right at the entrance to Hamstead Grange and, just here, there's a lovely vista across the Newtown River and the Solent towards Cowes. From here the road runs straight past Pennethorne Park Farm, rejoins your outward route just north of Pigeon Coo Farm Ⓐ, and comes to a fork 150 yds (137m) farther on.

Ⓓ Turn right here onto the Hamstead Trail, still signposted towards the Newport/Yarmouth road. Pass the farm on your right, and carry on until you reach a letterbox at a fork in the track. Follow the Hamstead Trail around to the left, continue for 250 yds (229m) to a bend in the road, then turn left onto footpath S9 towards Ningwood. The path follows the woodland edge and comes to a stile; go over, and bear left across an open field along the line of a rickety wire fence. Cross two stiles in quick succession, then follow the waymarked route across a narrow field and over a little iron-

Sailing in Newtown River

railed footbridge into Nunneys Wood.

Leave the woods at a stile, still following the path towards Ningwood. Continue down the side of an open field until you reach a stile in the corner, quite close to the road. Nip across, back to the car park where your walk began. ●

After more than 70 years, it's hard to decipher the worn lettering on the touching little memorial at **Hamstead Point**. The simple stone cross records the tragic deaths of three young men; the eldest, David Cox, was just 22 when he and his friend William Pollock were lost at sea off Hamstead Ledge in November 1932. Then, just 18 months later, Robin Cox suffered a similar fate.

19 *Calbourne and Winkle Street*

The walk sets out along the Tennyson Trail for the climb onto Mottistone Down, then continues through Brighstone Forest and across farmland towards Calbourne and Winkle Street. The homeward stretch heads south along Lynch Lane. A steep climb over Brighstone Down leads you back to the Tennyson Trail for a downhill stroll to the finishing line.

START Junction of Lynch Lane and Strawberry Lane, one mile north of Brighstone
DISTANCE 5½ miles (8.8km)
TIME 3 hours
PARKING Free at start
ROUTE FEATURES With two strenuous climbs, poor signposting and a dozen stiles, this walk isn't for the faint-hearted. Please lead dogs through farmland

Follow the signposted Forestry Commission Jubilee Trail from the car park gates, and walk up the prominent white track onto Mottistone Down. There are wide views to the Long Stone (see Walk 10) and the coast to your left, and you may see kestrels or buzzards soaring on the downland wind. Continue for just over ½ mile (805m), until the Jubilee Trail turns into the forest through a signposted gate.

Ⓐ Turn right through the gate and follow the bridleway down through the forest to a complex six-way junction. Think of it as a mini-roundabout, take the second exit left, and continue for 200 yds (183m) to the next junction. (*A tree-felling programme scheduled for winter 2003-04 may change the look of this area.*) Four broad tracks meet here; a few paces farther on, take the smaller, unsignposted bridleway that bears off to the right into the trees. The path leads gently down the hill, then crosses a wider track and swings to the right along the woodland edge.

Ⓑ Now the bridleway swings back

PUBLIC TRANSPORT Bus services to Brighstone and Calbourne (01983 532373)
REFRESHMENTS The Sun: real ale, baguettes, jacket potatoes, hot meals, garden
PUBLIC TOILETS None
ORDNANCE SURVEY MAPS Explorer OL29 (Isle of Wight)

The pretty row of cottages overlooking the Caul Bourne is an established island attraction. Originally called Barrington Row, the cottages have been known as **Winkle Street** for at least 50 years – though it's not certain how the name originated. You can see the **village sheepwash**, last used in the mid-1970s, about halfway down the stream opposite the cottages. The small brass plate fixed to the stonework tells you more about its history.

to the left and leads you out of the woods. Carry straight on along the edge of a field and continue onto a wide green lane with views towards Newtown River and the Solent. Soon the lane merges with a gravel road that swings in from your left, and continues to a fork in the track.

C Turn right, and follow the gravel road between the buildings at Westover Farm. The road bears left into Withybed Copse, then climbs gently and bears back to the right. Just here, look out for a way-marked stile in the trees on your left; nip across, and follow the path as it winds across wooden board-walks to a waymarked stile on the far edge of the woods. Cross this one, too, and continue across the open field towards the left-hand corner of the woods on the skyline.

Two more waymarked stiles carry you across a farm track and the path continues between wire fences. Another six stiles lead you through the fields to a plank bridge over a brook. Bear right here across the corner of a small field to a stile between two metal gates; nip over, and follow the right-hand field edge to a final gate and stile that leads you out onto the B4301 at Calbourne.

D Cross over, turn right, and follow the narrow left-hand verge to the crossroads for a well-earned break at The Sun. Turn right here down Lynch Lane, signposted towards Winkle Street, and *keep an eye open for cars as there's no pavement along this road*. Pass All Saints' Church, set back on the green on your left, then bear left past Winkle Street and the gates of Westover Park. Continue for 650 yds (594m) to a small Southern Water building on your left; then, 100 yds (91m) later, look out for the signposted bridleway CB20 on your left.

Winkle Street

E Turn left up the tree-shaded track towards Brighstone Forest and the Tennyson Trail. After just 200 yds (183m), follow the bridleway as it swings off to the right through a waymarked metal gate and begins the long climb onto Brighstone Down. You've every excuse to stop for a breather, for behind you there's an unfolding panorama that stretches right across Newtown harbour and the Solent to the New Forest.

At the top right-hand corner of the long field, the bridleway dives through a small wooden gate into the shade of Brighstone Forest – but the climb isn't over yet. Just keep straight on through the long avenue of beech trees and zigzag right, then left, at the first forest crossroads. The trees are younger here, and the forest clearings bright with willow herb.

The English Channel rises into view as you reach the summit; look away left here to the Ordnance Survey triangulation pillar which marks the end of your 500-ft (152m) climb from the road. Keep

> *What is the bench mark number on the Ordnance Survey triangulation pillar on Brighstone Down?*

> The **concrete column** on Brighstone Down is one of around 6,500 Ordnance Survey 'triangulation pillars' that, until very recently, formed the basic framework for all Ordnance Survey mapping. Now, the advent of satellite-based global positioning systems has transformed map-making technology and consigned most of these hilltop pillars to the history books. The 'bench mark' on the side of the pillar is used to fix its height above sea level.

straight on past the turning to the pillar, across the scrubby heathland of gorse, heather, holly and stunted beech trees. Now, simply follow the track as it drops off the summit and continues to a junction marked by a four-way signpost.

F Turn right here onto the Tennyson Trail, and continue across the next junction towards the Brighstone/Calbourne Road. Follow the gravel road as it bears right and leaves the forest at a wooden gate, then turn to the right as the Tennyson Trail joins the Old Highway towards Mottistone Down. This is the homeward straight, and there are great views for most of the way as the track drops gently down to Lynch Lane. At the road, zigzag briefly left and right to return to the starting point of the walk. ●

20 *Steaming into Havenstreet*

START Firestone Copse car park.
DISTANCE 5½ miles (8.8km)
TIME 3 hours
PARKING Free Forestry Commission car park at the start
ROUTE FEATURES This walk includes a dozen stiles and a mile of walking on country lanes, making it less suitable for groups or families with children. Please lead dogs along the roads, as well as through the farms

After setting off through mixed Forestry Commission woodlands, the walk continues through Havenstreet village and past the steam railway centre. Now the route threads its way along a wooded bridleway and across open fields to Rowlands Lane. The homeward trek follows this quiet country lane north, before branching off across farmland and back through Havenstreet for a woodland finale.

Leave the car park between the picnic tables and set off down the gravelled path to the woods. Continue for 250 yds (229m), then turn right and follow the path along the woodland edge for another 100 yds (91m) as far as the stile on your left. Nip across, then zigzag left and right over a second stile onto the narrow, signposted path as it pulls clear of the woods along the edge of a couple of fields. At length the path bears left and briefly follows a gravelled driveway before reaching the village road opposite Holmdale House old folk's home.

Ⓐ Turn right, pass the White Hart and the impressive Northbrooke House nursing home Ⓑ, and follow the village road under the railway bridge to Havenstreet station. *Take care along this section, as there's only a short length of pavement.*

PUBLIC TRANSPORT Isle of Wight steam railway trains (01983 882204) connect Havenstreet with the Island Line at Smallbrook Junction. Limited bus service from Newport and Ryde (01983 532373)
REFRESHMENTS The White Hart: Real ales, meals, lunchtime snacks, family garden; Havenstreet Station cafeteria: teas, coffees, lunches, ice creams
PICNIC/PLAY AREA There are picnic areas at the start, and at Havenstreet Station
PUBLIC TOILETS For pub and railway patrons only
ORDNANCE SURVEY MAPS Explorer OL29 (Isle of Wight)

Near Pondcast Farm

The Isle of Wight steam railway has all the ingredients for a great family day out. At Havenstreet you'll find beautifully restored station buildings straight out of the 1920s, as well as a museum, souvenir shop, and licensed refreshment room. There's a recreation field, too, where you're welcome to picnic or enjoy your own ball games. But, of course, the main attraction is the vintage steam trains that puff through Havenstreet on most days between April and September. Your ticket buys unlimited travel for the day, and there are special fares for families.

C About 75 yds (69m) beyond the station entrance, fork left onto bridleway N18 towards Combley and Arreton Down. A quiet, leafy stretch ushers in just over a mile of easy walking as you follow the bridleway all the way to Combley Farm. Follow the track as it bears left, then right, through the farmyard and continue for another 100 yds (91m).

D Double back through the waymarked wicket gate on your left, and head diagonally towards the top left-hand corner of the small field. Bear left at the metal field gate, follow the track along the left-hand edge of this large open field, and continue into the next field through a gap in the

Railway preservation is a way of life on the Isle of Wight. The network once boasted more than 55 miles (89km) of track – but, faced with high summer demand and few low season passengers, local railway companies cut their costs by running second-hand trains bought cheaply from the mainland. The tradition still continues, with old London Underground carriages running the electrified service between Ryde and Shanklin.

hedge. Almost at the far side of this second field, the track swings left through a metal gate; leave it here, and follow the bridleway as it bears right towards a similar gate 100 yds (91m) ahead of you. From here, follow the waymarked route across the middle of the next field to the metal gates on the far side. There's a farm crossroads here, and your way lies along the bridleway straight ahead.

E Continue along the waymarked track as it zigzags left and right past Duxmore Farm. Although the bridleway downgrades to a footpath here, it follows a wide farm lane with grass along the centre. Continue past a field gate and stile, and follow a line of wooden electricity poles across the middle of an open field. A small wooden gate on the far side of the field leads you to a waymarked

T-junction. Turn left, nip over the stile beside Little Duxmore, then turn right and follow the wider farm track leading out onto Rowlands Lane.

F Turn left onto the road, pass the attractive Rowlands Farm on your right, and continue for ¾ mile (1.2km) to the railway bridge. *There's no pavement here so, although traffic is usually light, do take care and watch out for the occasional car.*

G Just beyond the bridge, turn left over the stile at Bridge Farm onto footpath R9. Two more stiles follow in quick succession; now, follow the footpath towards the far left-hand corner of the field, where you'll find a stile set deep in the hedge at the entrance to a small wood. Jump the stile, and follow the narrow woodland path to a footbridge and stile. Cross over, then bear left through the next field to a double stile at the top left-hand corner. Nip across, turn left along the short side of a long thin field to another pair of stiles, and continue beside the hedge on your left to yet another stile straight ahead. Go over this one, too, continuing up the gravelled drive past Ivy Dene to Havenstreet village.

B Turn right, and follow the road past the White Hart as far as the telephone box on your left. Turn left here, and retrace your outward steps back to the start.

? *What is the height restriction under Havenstreet railway bridge?*

Havenstreet station has been the home of the Isle of Wight **steam railway** for more than 30 years. Five years after British Railways closed the line in 1966, the company began restoring the track, buildings and trains. A new terminus was opened at Wootton in 1986, and by 1991 the rails once again stretched eastwards through Ashey to Smallbrook Junction. With its **Victorian locomotives and carriages**, the line is now one of Britain's premier heritage railways.

Steaming into Havenstreet WALK 20

Further Information

Walking Safety

Always take with you both warm and waterproof clothing and sufficient food and drink. Wear suitable footwear, i.e. strong walking boots or shoes that give a good grip over stony ground, on slippery slopes and in muddy conditions. Try to obtain a local weather forecast and bear it in mind before you start. Do not be afraid to abandon your proposed route and return to your starting point in the event of a sudden and unexpected deterioration in the weather.

All the walks described in this book will be safe to do, given due care and respect, even during the winter. Indeed, a crisp, fine winter day often provides perfect walking conditions, with firm ground underfoot and a clarity of light unique to that time of the year.

The most difficult hazard likely to be encountered is mud, especially when walking along woodland and field paths, farm tracks and bridleways – the latter in particular can often get churned up by cyclists and horses. In summer, an additional difficulty may be narrow and overgrown paths, particularly along the edges of cultivated fields. Neither should constitute a major problem provided that the appropriate footwear is worn.

Follow the Country Code

- Enjoy the countryside and respect its life and work
- Guard against all risk of fire
- Take your litter home
- Fasten all gates
- Help to keep all water clean
- Keep your dogs under control
- Protect wildlife, plants and trees
- Keep to public paths across farmland
- Take special care on country roads
- Leave livestock, crops and machinery alone
- Make no unnecessary noise
- Use gates and stiles to cross fences, hedges and walls
                (The Countryside Agency)

Useful Contacts

Blackgang Chine
Blackgang Chine, near Ventnor, Isle of Wight
PO38 2HN
Tel: 01983 730052

Blackgang Chine

Brading Roman Villa
Morton Old Road, Brading,
Isle of Wight PO36 0EN
Tel: 01983 406223

Campaign to Protect Rural England
128 Southwark Street,
London SE1 0SW
Tel: 020 7981 2800

Countryside Agency
John Dower House, Crescent Place, Cheltenham GL50 3RA
Tel: 01242 521381

English Heritage
Customer Services Department,
PO Box 569, Swindon SN2 2YP
Tel: 0870 333 1181

English Nature
Hampshire & Isle of Wight Team,
1 Southampton Road,
Lyndhurst, Hants SO43 7BU
Tel: 023 8028 6410

Forestry Commission
Parkhurst Forest, Newport,
Isle of Wight PO30 5UL
Tel: 01420 23666

Fort Victoria Country Park
Fort Victoria, Yarmouth,
Isle of Wight
Tel: 01983 823893

Isle of Wight Council
Rights of Way Department,
Engineering Services,
Jubilee Stores,
The Quay,
Isle of Wight PO30 2EH
Tel: 01983 823777

Isle of Wight Donkey Sanctuary
Lower Winstone Farm,
Wroxall,
Isle of Wight PO38 3AA
Tel: 01983 852693

Isle of Wight Steam Railway
The Railway Station, Havenstreet,
Isle of Wight PO33 4DS
Tel: 01983 882204

Isle of Wight Tourism
Westridge Centre, Brading Road,
Ryde, Isle of Wight PO33 1QS
Tel: 01983 813818

**Hampshire & Isle of Wight
Wildlife Trust**
Woodside House, Woodside Road,
Eastleigh, Hants SO50 4ET
Tel: 023 8061 3636

National Rail Enquiries
Tel: 08457 48 49 50

The National Trust
PO Box 39, Bromley,
Kent BR1 3XL
Tel: 0870 458 4000

Isle of Wight Donkey Sanctuary

Tennyson's Monument

Nunwell House
Coach Lane, Brading, Isle of Wight
Tel: 01983 407240

The Needles Pleasure Park
The Needles, Alum Bay,
Isle of Wight PO39 0JD
Tel: 0870 458 0022

Ordnance Survey
Romsey Road, Southampton
SO16 4GU
Tel: 08456 05 05 05

Red Funnel Ferries
Tel: 0870 444 8898

Royal Society for the Protection of Birds
The Lodge, Sandy, Beds SG19 2DL
Tel: 01767 680551

St Catherine's Lighthouse
Niton, Ventnor, Isle of Wight
Tel: 01983 867979

Southern Vectis
Tel: 01983 532373

WightLink Ferries
Tel: 0870 582 7744

The Woodland Trust
Autumn Park, Grantham, Lincs
NG31 6LL
Tel: 01476 581111

Ordnance Survey Maps
Explorer OL 29 (Isle of Wight)

Answers to Questions

Walk 1: The wireless pioneer, Guglielmo Marconi. The first wireless transmission was made from the warship *HMS Vernon* to Marconi's wireless station at Knowles Farm in 1901. The message was from an officer on board the ship to the daughter of Mr Kirkpatrick at Knowles Farm, inviting her to lunch. Later that year Marconi transmitted the first long-distance wireless message from Knowles Farm to Brean Down in Cornwall, another NT property.

Walk 2: One shilling (5p) a year.

Walk 3: The church is dedicated to St John the Evangelist.

Walk 4: All these species are found at the Norton Spit Site of Special Scientific Interest.

Walk 5: 1928.

Walk 6: More than 2000.

Walk 7: The Tennyson Memorial was erected on the site of the old beacon in 1897.

Walk 8: £200.

Walk 9: The gate was built in memory of William Sells, Rector of Niton between 1890 and 1918.

Walk 10: The churchyard is mown annually at the end of July, after the wild flowers and grasses have seeded.

Walk 11: The trenches were dug during the Second World War to stop enemy gliders from landing on the Down.

Walk 12: The name is probably Saxon, and is believed to mean 'Alfred's Farm'.

Walk 13: Rev Stobart was the vicar of Carisbrooke, 1902-1914.

Walk 14: August 1998.

Walk 15: Mrs E Smith, of Mill Farm, Bembridge, in 1958.

Walk 16: Ryde.

Walk 17: No parking is allowed within 250 ft (76m).

Walk 18: The last collection is at 10am, Monday to Friday.

Walk 19: OSBM S2492.

Walk 20: 13ft 6in (4.1m).

The Nodes Beacon replica